RIVIERA MAYA

MEXICO YUCATAN

CANCUN

THE VERY BEST OF

MICHAEL FRIEDEL

TEXT BY MARION FRIEDEL

EDITION MM

This is the land of the pheasant and the deer and Mayab is its name.... In 1517, when the Spaniard Francisco Hernández de Córdoba first set foot on the peninsula, he came upon some indigenous fishermen. When he asked them who owned the country and what its name was, they replied: "M'ac ubab t'han," which means "We do not understand your words." But the Spaniard thought they had said "Yucatán" and so he gave the land this new name. The large flat peninsula, which separates the Gulf of Mexico from the turquoise-coloured Caribbean, is an important part of the Mundo Mayo - the world of the Mayas - and belongs to Mexico. Since the Spanish "misunderstanding" it has gained further names. Today the peninsula is divided into three federal Mexican states: Yucatán, Campeche and Quintana Roo. The low-lying, marshy land of Campeche and Yucatán, dotted with lagoons along the Gulf coast, offers little to tempt bathers. However, Quintana Roo on the Caribbean side has drawn a trump-card. Every superlative, all the magical elements of a tropical coastline come together here - with its offshore islets, crystal-clear seas, from turquoise to ultramarine, protective coral reefs and gleaming white, powder-fine coral sand. Quintana Roo, with its tourist metropolis of Cancún, is currently being turned into a gigantic leisure-park; and the marketing-men have christened its picture-book coasts the "Mayan Riviera" and "Costa Maya."

The team responsible for this book, photographer Michael Friedel and his journalist wife Marion, are both internationally renowned and have produced books about many dreamislands of the world. Their illustrated books include *The Maldives*, *The Seychelles*, *Mauritius* and *Bali*. Now, in a series on peninsulas or "half-islands" the Dominican Republic is joined Yucatán.

Someone else who has seen most of the world is travel expert Knut Wehner. Since 1988 he has been an honorarycitizen of Cancún. He foresees a rosy future for the tourist development of the Yucatán peninsula. "If it is true that by the year 2000 tourism will be the leading business sector, then Yucatán and the Caribbean coast of Mexico must be one of the biggest and most important travel destinations in the world." Mexican planners and international investors are making sure this happens, but above all it will be due to the unique combination of holiday variety, pure Caribbean conditions and Mayan culture. Bathing holidays on one of the endless beaches, staying in a new luxury hotel complex, and an exciting journey to discover the sacred sites of the Mayas, some of which date back to 2000 B.C. Here the dry details of history come fascinatingly to life. More and more temple complexes are being uncovered in the virgin forest. Almost daily these ruins, many thousands of years old, reveal new secrets about a unique and impressive civilization.

Mexico and the Mundo Maya have had a strong influence of the life of Angelika Erdmann. When studying archaeology at the Irvine campus of the University of California, she chose Mayan culture as her specialist subject. As a tour-guide for two years she came to know Mexico better than her own German homeland. She has written a guidebook: Mexico - Myths, Markets and Mestizos, and her varied and practical experience also provides the basis of the information section of this book.

Michael Friedel
Knut Wehner
Angelika Erdmann

NOTE ON THE ILLUSTRATIONS

PUNTA MAROMA, the spit of land near PUERTO MORELOS, lies between CANCÚN and PLAYA DEL CARMEN. Snuggling deep in the virgin vegetation which surrounds it, stands a small, exclusive hotel complex - the CASA MAROMA. A 2km-wide belt of virgin forest and mangroves separates the new 4-lane Mex 307 expressway from the almost deserted and undeveloped Caribbean shore.
Pages 8-9

Sunrise over TULUM, which was once probably called ZAMÁ - City of Dawn. It is the only Mayan city which is perched on a cliff high above the Caribbean Sea. From 1000 AD to 1550 the bay at the foot of the Temple of the Wind God served as a harbour for the once important trading centre. Also, from here women visited the island of Cozumel where they worshipped their fertility-goddess, Ixchel.
Pages 10-11

The beaches of the RIVIERA MAYA stretch for 150 km (90 miles) from Cancún to Tulum. The LAS PALAPAS hotel is on the Playa del Carmen beach. PALAPAS is the name given to the traditional palm roofs of Mayan huts, which are supported on four posts. They have given their name to this eco-hotel with its two-storied chalets. For building, the fresh or dried leaves of the indigenous huano palm are used. Pages 12-13

In the archaeological and snorkelling park of CHANKA-NAAB on the island of COZUMEL hundreds of people go snorkelling every day. They are mostly cruise-ship passengers. surrounded by thousand's of reef-dwelling fish, which are fed with tortillas. COZUMEL with over 20 reefs of various sizes, is among the best diving areas in the Caribbean. In the wake of Jacques Cousteau, who was the first man to explore the reefs in 1961, over 1000 diving-schools now offer their services. Pages 14-15

The beach of PLAYA DEL CARMEN in front of the EL FARO hotel and the BLUE PARROT BAR. Until a few years ago the beaches of Quintana Roo and the Caribbean coast of Mexico were deserted except for a few scattered fishing communities. The aboriginal population, the MAYAS, chiefly live as peasant farmers in the interior of the peninsula. They are scarcely, if at all, involved in the tourist boom along the coast. Words by Marion Friedel. Pages 16-19

The 7-mile stretch of sand running from PUNTA CANCUN to PUNTA NIZUC is one of the world's longest hotel-lined beaches. Here you will find no sign of "sleeping policemen", the improvised obstacles in the road, intended to slow traffic down to a walking pace. But when you are touring cross-country, they provide an opportunity for the many street hawkers to make a bit of money. That is why, for every official topes or traffic-calmer, you will usually see four or five private ones behind it. Text: Marion Friedel. Pages 20-23

Since first light the radio beacon in the EL FARO hotel's private lighthouse has closed down and will not operate again until sunset as an official guide to shipping in the narrow straits between PLAYA DEL CARMEN and COZUMEL. The earliest guests are taking their morning bathe on the still empty beach, where soon a colourful crowd of international sunworshippers as well as many Mexicans will be romping. Pages 24-25

The modern luxury hotel complexes on the Riviera Maya are a very recent phenomenon and none were built before the late 1990s. In PLAYA DEL CARMEN, unlike the big complexes in CANCÚN, you will find mainly smaller, individual hotels. EL FARO's turquoise-blue freshwater pool, with its deep shadows, reflects the unique play of colours in the Caribbean Sea. Pages 26-27.

NOTE ON THE ILLUSTRATIONS

Imagination knows no bounds. The language of pictures is international and the purchase of paint is usually the first and often the only investment made by someone planning to start a new life. People flock from all over Mexico to seek work in PLAYA DEL CARMEN, where they can earn a living in the new hotels, bars, restaurants and shops that are opening every day, though admittedly they are paid only the minimum legal wage. Pages 28-29

A nursery school in COLOSIO, the district of poor settlers: waiters, bartenders, chamber-maids, bricklayers and musicians - who have come with their families from all over Mexico looking for work. In a spirit of get-up-and-go they arrive in their tens of thousands on the coast of the Riviera Maya, to work and make a better future for themselves. They occupy large areas of the connurbation of PLAYA DEL CARMEN illegally, but with the support of local politicians. Pages 30-31

PUNTA CANCÚN, the northernmost point of the 21km (13 miles) long island of CANCÚN which is only 400m wide at its widest point. The ZONA TURISTICA comprises, in addition to its giant hotels, a congress centre, a disco centre and a shopping centre. It was in 1969 that this "test-tube" holiday resort was designed on the drawing-board and then realized and developed by the Mexicans into the world's must successful tourist complex. Pages 32-33

COZUMEL, the island where it all began. Since 1927 it has had regular air connections with the USA. In the mid-1950s the first hotel was opened and in the 1960s the cruise-ships arrived. By the early 1970s international tourism was well on its way. In recent years COZUMEL has become the capital of Caribbean cruising, with moorings for 9 ships at a time, or over 800 per year. Pages 34-35

MÉRIDA was the first Spanish settlement in Yucatán. Thanks to a boom in sisal it was one of the richest cities in Mexico until the 1930s - but after that it became one of the poorest. Only with the explosive development of tourism on the coasts of Yucatán has Mérida experienced a new commercial revival. Every Sunday, outside the town hall, folk-dance groups recall the good old, prosperous days. Pages 36-37

After the Spanish conquest in the 16th century the 1600 km (960 mile) long coast of Yucatán was almost uninhabited. Today the tourist centres throb to the FIESTA MEXICANA, a veritable circus of entertainments, an artificial blend of all the varied cultures and traditions of the vast land of Mexico. Every day turns into a FIESTA MEXICANA with tequila, sangria and tortillas; with mariachi music and with flamenco, rock and pop. Pages 38-39

When CANCÚN was still no more than an uninhabited coral bank, the fishermen's island ISLA MUJERES was already a holiday resort for Mexicans and a well-kept secret among globetrotters. Today it is the most popular day-trip destination for tourists from CANCÚN. They arrive by ferry, speed-boat or "pirate ship," or on a replica of Columbus' flagship, the Pinta. In the evening, when the last ferry has left the island, the place returns again to being a tranquil little village. Pages 40-41

The beaches south of TULUM are some of the most fabled in the world. Until a few years ago TULUM was only known for its famous temple complex. The picturesque, rustic huts of EL MIRADOR, roofed with palm-fronds, and with sand floors and hammocks, were a secret known only to a few adventurous tourists. Today, more and more small individual hotels and posadas are springing up along this picturesque coast, with its wide sandy beaches. Pages 42-43

NOTE ON THE ILLUSTRATIONS

In the year 1518 members of the first Spanish expeditionary force were sailing along the coast when, to their astonishment, they discovered a city: "so large that we could not have thought the city of Seville itself to be larger or finer....We saw a very tall tower..." At this period TULUM was still a bustling, densely populated city. Today the fortified city only comes to life at certain times, from 7am to 5pm daily. Pages 44-45

The pink sand beach of XPU HA stretches for miles along the RIVIERA MAYA. The beach is still a breeding-ground for sea-turtles. A base for blue-water fishing and a bathing resort popular with Mexican families, it has little beach-huts selling freshly caught fish. But a new development is under way. A club hotel has been built, and a theme park, the socalled Eco-Nature Park, is attracting thousands of visitors. Pages 46-47

A sandy trail winds for 50 km (30 miles) from TULUM to PUNTA ALLEN, the tip of a narrow promontory. On one side lonely beaches and the Caribbean surf, on the other, wide lagoons and mangrove forests. The road leads to the big SIAN KA'AN BIOSPHERE RESERVE, which has been a protected area for flora and fauna since 1986. At BOCA PAILA the green waters of the lagoons flow into the turquoise-blue sea. Pages 48-49

CHICHÉN ITZÁ and its pyramid of KUKULKÁN (the Plumed Serpent). The 24m (79 ft) high pyramid conceals a deep cosmic symbolism. Twice a year, at the equinox, it is the scene of a phenomenon that was only discovered 20 years ago: the form of a snake which, in the shifting pattern of light and shade, appears to wriggle down the pyramid, ending at a stone serpent's head. Pages 50-51.

Increasing numbers of people, especially Mexicans, make their way to CHICHÉN ITZÁ during the equinoctial days of 21-22 March and 22-23 September. The nine-tiered pyramid, built as long ago as 800 A.D., then becomes a source of cosmic energy for New Agers. Over 40,000 mainly white-clad visitors lean against the sun-heated blocks of stone, drawing new supplies of energy for health and a long life. Pages 52-53

The original statue of the rain-god CHAC-MOOL lies on the plinth of the Temple of the Warriors in CHICHÉN ITZá. In the CHANKANAAB lagoon on COZUMEL the rain-god was submerged in 4m (12 ft) of water, beside a stone table bearing Mayan hieroglyphics. Together with a statue of the Virgin Mary and a figure of Christ, they are a profitable attraction for snorkellers. On land a small park dotted with replicas provides a beginners' guide to the pre-Columbian culture of Mexico. Pages 54-55

The Mayan city of UXMAL with its 38m (123ft) high TEMPLE OF THE MAGICIANS. To climb the 118 steep steps you need to be in good condition and not prone to vertigo. Here visitors can still look at a 1,000-year-old building, experience its mysterious history at close quarters and touch it with their own hands. However, as the flood of tourists increases, "No Entry" is the rule in more and more of the pyramids. Pages 56-57

UXMAL is currently one of the largest archaeological excavations. So far only a small area has been exposed. The entrance fees are being used to finance a series of new digs. The Mexican archaeologists are assisted in the main by Mayas, who work with dexterity and patience, showing great pride and respect for the fascinating riddle of their mysterious past. Pages 58-59

NOTE ON THE ILLUSTRATIONS

KOHUNLICH with its great mask (400-600 A.D.) lies in dense jungle on the border with Belize and was not discovered until 1912. Deep in the rain-forest near TULUM lie the ruins of what was once the great Mayan city of COBA. Only by following narrow jungle paths can you reach the "Nohoch Mul", the highest pyramid in the Yucatán. Its 120 steps reach a height of 138 ft. Pages 60-61

The GRAND CENOTE, between Tulum and Coba, is an entrance to the subterranean river system of the SAC ACTUN. Divers from Aquatech, in Villas Derosa, explore the watercourse between strange-looking stalactites and stalagmites. A stretch of 4328m (over a quarter-mile) of the 17.4 m (57ft) deep river has been mapped in recent years. The divers require special training and a cave-diving certificate. Pages 62-63

The CENOTE of XKEKEN in Dzitnup near Valladolid. The entrance starts in a low narrow cave and ends in an imposing limestone cavern. The sun's rays fall through two small holes in the roof on to the clear water of the underground lake. Small fish swim in the cool water and bathing is allowed. These subterranean rivers and lakes were the main source of drinking-water for ancient Yucatán and still are today. Pages 64-65

The ROYAL TOUCAN lives within the bounds of the XCARET Ecological Park, representing the species in the wild. Several large wildlife parks have been created along the Riviera Maya. They are well laid-out, enclosed areas for flora, fauna and indigenous Mexican cultures. On payment of a substantial entrance-fee the thousands of visitors are offered a programmed adventure experience in a well-tended wilderness - guaranteed risk-free. Pages 66-67

The jungle near TRES GARANTÍAS in southern Quintana Roo was once densely populated and heavily cultivated. Evidence of this history is found in imposing Mayan ruins and the remains of a large church. In their effort to stamp out paganism the Spanish also wiped out the pagan population. This landscape is now deserted, the trackless woods are now only visited by chicleros and foresters. Pages 68-69

Traditional slash-and-burn clearance of a MILPA, land reclaimed from the jungle for planting the staple crops of maize, beans and pumpkins, near the Mayan village of SAN FRANCISCO AKÉ. Archaeologists are mystified as to why the civilization of the Mayas collapsed and their cities were gradually abandoned in the course of the centuries. Was it due to ecological catastrophes, disease or war? Pages 70-71

An Easter procession in SAN FRANCISCO AKÉ. The Mayas are 90% Catholic but still preserve the nature-worship of their ancestors. The women in their HUIPILES, colourfully embroidered white dresses, bake TORTILLAS twice a day over an open fire. These little pancakes made from maize-flour are the basis of every meal. The Mayas call themselve "The Maize People" and their life is built around the cultivation of this crop. Pages 72-73

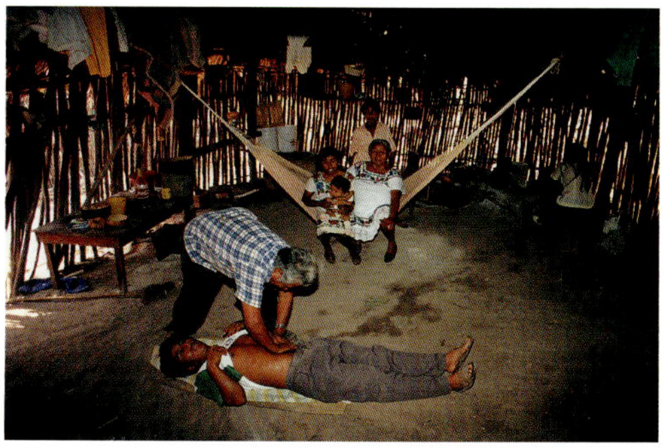

In the home of JUAN JOSÉ ITZÁ, a descendant of the proud ITZÁ tribe, who defended their kingdom against the Spanish until 1697 - the last people of the Yucatán to be conquered. He and his brother are the most famous CURANDEROS or natural healers in Quintana Roo. Their very effective form of medicine consists, in part, of over 800 active extracts from the rich flora and fauna of the jungle of Yucatán - God's secret pharmacy. Pages 74-75

NOTE ON THE ILLUSTRATIONS

BACALAR and LAS LAGUNAS DE SIETE COLORES, the "lagoons of seven colours" set in the green bush-landscape of southern Yucatán. The little township with its fort, built in 1733, was once an important Spanish settlement and military stronghold. The big fresh-water lake, with its 90m (300ft) deep CENOTE AZUL, is a favourite weekend resort for the inhabitants of Chetumal, the provincial capital. Pages 76-77

The name FLAMINGO comes from the Spanish word flamenco - the fiery music of Andalusia. It aptly describes the breathtaking sight of a soaring, vivid pink cloud as hundreds of flamingos take off from the water. In the LAGUNA RIO LAGARTOS, on the northerly point of the Yucatán peninsula, up to 30,000 flamingos nest at the start of the rainy season, from June to August. Yucatán is home to the world's largest flamingo colony. Pages 78-79

The BANCO CHINCHORRO off the COSTA MAYA, at the southern end of Quintana Roo, is part of the fifth largest barrier-reef in the world. The coral reef, swarming with fish, lies 26 km (16 miles) from the little fishing-village of XCALAK, on the peninsula of the same name, and is visited chiefly by lobster fishermen. In their boats scuba-divers can reach a world-class diving paradise and plumb the deep fissures of the outer reef. Pages 80-81

The island of HOLBOX forms the northernmost point of the state of Quintana Roo and of the Yucatán peninsula. With an area of only 32 sq km (12 sq miles), it consists mainly of mangrove swamps. It was originally a pirate haunt and until the end of the last century sailors collected timber here. Today the few hundred inhabitants of HOLBOX make a living from fishing and selling handwoven hammocks. Pages 82-83

The PINTA, an authentic replica of one Columbus' three Spanish caravels, at anchor off the bird-sanctuary of ISLA CONTOY. The island is a nesting-place for thousands of sea-birds including frigatebirds, cormorants and pelicans. Ships must obtain special permission to anchor there overnight. A limited number of nature-lovers can make a day-trip to CONTOY, organized by Colón Tours of Cancún. Pages 84-85

RIVIERA MAYA and COSTA MAYA are new names for holiday areas along the coast of QUINTANA ROO. Deserted, unspoilt beaches alternate with large, ultramodern tourist developments. In PLAYA DEL CARMEN, on the RIVIERA MAYA, a mixture of large hotel complexes and numerous individual hotels has grown up. Knut Wehner writes about the unique holiday attraction of the Yucatán, which blends Mayan culture with the essence of the Caribbean. Pages 86-89

The authors, Marion and Michael Friedel spent 4 months travelling around Yucatán. Since their first visit together 30 years ago a great deal has changed, especially in tourism. That is why they made it their task to revisit the most important regions of the peninsula, to soak up the atmosphere and take photographs. They travelled by minibus, single-engined Cessna, helicopter and boat. The Michael Friedel workshop. Pages 90-91

On the final pages:

GENERAL INFORMATION
USEFUL TIPS
CLIMATIC TABLES
BOOKS OF DISCOVERY AND TRAVEL
MAP
PUBLISHING DETAILS
Pages 92-96

Bruce Montes jumps off his bicycle and, when everyone else is aboard the 4-seater Cessna, he squeezes in behind the joystick, starts the engine and prepares to take off on an excursion flight. He does not have far to go to work: the little airstrip lies in the middle of the Playacar holiday centre with its big, international, all-inclusive hotel complexes, a golf-course, a smart residential area and the Avenida 30, the main street of Playa del Carmen. This once insignificant fishing-village, whose only claim to fame was its ferry service to the island of Cozumel, has now developed into an Eldorado, a multi-cultural playground, and the fastest growing city in the whole of Mexico. We fly low over roofs, dusty roads and countless building sites. Then we cross the white sands and soar out over the turquoise-blue sea. To right and left, as far as the eye can see, the coast stretches away in a seemingly endless chain of wide, curving bays, edged with gleaming white sand, with waters ranging in colour from pale peacock blue to ultramarine. The Caribbean coast, over 400 km (240 miles) long, divides into two parts, to which the marketing men have given the hard-selling names "Riviera Maya" and "Costa Maya."

As the Cessna slowly gains altitude, the vast coastal infrastructure itself - the motorway, leisure centres, hotels, a deep-water harbour and the square parcels of development land - all dwindle to insignificant white lines and patches amid the grey-green cladding of impenetrable jungle, dense bush and mangrove forests, which covers the peninsula like a carpet and from which every square yard of land for building or agriculture must be wrested.

As we land again in Playa, everything which appeared from the air to be organized and tidily divided into rectangular plots, lapses once more into a delightful atmosphere of creative chaos, of "What the heck, let's do it!" Here in Playa optimism predominates, imagination blossoms, yet everything is unfinished; there are great tracts of nothingness and holes in the dusty, coral-sand roads.

Miguel remembers with horror his first nights in Playa. He had set up the posts for his hammock in the middle of a large, bare building-plot measuring 210 sq meters (a mere twentieth of an acre) which he occupied in the Colonia Donaldo Colosio. Trembling with fear he lay in his hammock, his hands firmly grasping a machete, continuously on the lookout to defend his plot against sinister prowlers and drunken riff-raff. After all, he was just one of today's sixty thousand illegal settlers who have migrated here from every part of Mexico to find a better job in Playa. Miguel has found work in a hotel; a little hut stands on his plot of land, a roof for himself and his family of three. Life for them still lacks any electricity, water or sewerage. It is a struggle for survival in the face of poverty, disease and dirt.

For fair-haired Sabine from Germany, known locally as "La Rubia" (The Blonde), today is a black day. She is waiting impatiently at the hotel bar for her attorney and shaking with anger and disgust. A Mexican, who had been a good friend, has just relieved her of US$ 3,000. His plan was to purchase for her a uniquely desirable piece of land in Colosio, which foreigners were not allowed to buy, since it is against the law. It measured 210 sq meters and the price was US$2,300. Sabine is bitterly disappointed, particularly in her so-called friend, since so far she has not even got back the $700 change. Even so, says Sabine, she is having the time of her life and - something she particularly emphasizes - she has finally found her true self. A former air-hostess, Sabine loves the climate, the music and the people. Two years ago she chose to make Playa her new home, realizing it was the ideal place for her: "In Germany we had too much of everything. But here in Playa you can concentrate on the essentials of life. After all, when you get right down to it, what does a human being actually need...?"

In Playa del Carmen there are still no rigid rules and regulations to hamper people's creative urges, and a virtually free rein is given to fantasy; this is what draws rich and poor - mainly Europeans - to this place. They make grand plans and often invest every penny they have in a new future. Heinz, another German, sold his bar and his house in Mallorca and put all his money and mental energy, as well as that of his wife and children, into the construction of a hotel. He has planned it and thought it out entirely himself. Only the best is good enough. Heinz is a perfectionist and after two years' work the hotel is still only a shell. According to malicious gossip, his Mexican builders cannot do anything right. They say he does not want to see the project completed. Heinz is afraid that tourists will simply defile his dream-palace.

New restaurants are springing up like mushrooms and nearly always reflect the nationality of their owners. Trained chefs are a rarity. A German car-mechanic has gone into wurst; the Italians all boil spaghetti and bake pizzas; there's a Swiss serving rösti and fondue. The French restaurants are twice as expensive as the others. But nothing stays the same for long and the South African "Zulu" restaurant cooks Thai food.

We are now driving southward: to right and left of us tarantulas lie squashed flat on the road! The bush landscape we are passing through offers little variety. The Yucatán is a broad, flat limestone plateau with mangrove swamps and dry forests. But the initial impression of monotony is deceptive. The peninsula has a great wealth of hidden treasures, both natural and cultural. The jungle is not an untouched, primeval forest; it is a landscape that was once cultivated and exploited by a civilized society, but is now wild and overgrown. In the Chronicle of Yucatán, written in 1566 by the Spanish Franciscan monk, Diego de Landa, the decline and fall of the city of Mayapán in 1461 is described in the following words: "For over twenty years the inhabitants lived in prosperity and plenty, and they multiplied so greatly that the whole country seemed like a single town; in those days temples were built in such great numbers as one still sees everywhere today, and when one travels through the forests, one sees townships with wonderfully constructed houses and public buildings among the clusters of trees. This happy period ended at six o'clock one winter's evening, when a wind gradually blew up until it became a hurricane... This storm brought down tall trees, destroyed wild animals in great numbers, caused every large house to collapse and fires to spread out of control, so that the majority of the people either perished in the flames or were crushed by falling timber... And thus the country lost its former name of "Land of the deer and the pheasant". So many trees were lost that those which now remain look as if they had all been planted at the same time, since they are all of the same height. As soon as one looks out across the land from a higher point, one has the impression that it has been trimmed with shears." The monk also records: "With rivers and springs nature has dealt very differently here than in other countries. For the rivers and springs which everywhere else in the world flow on the surface of the earth are all hidden in this country in caverns beneath the earth. This was revealed to us because almost the whole coastline is full of freshwater springs rising out of the sea-bed. It is possible to draw water from them in many places when the tide has ebbed, leaving the shore almost dry. In the interior Our Lord has provided a number of water-holes, which the Indios call Cenotes. They lie in hollowed-out rocks which descend to the water; ...and all flow into the sea. These cenotes contain remarkably clear water..inside they have beautiful vaulted roofs of fine rock..."

This large and complex subterranean network of rivers and caves was formed by rain-water seeping through the porous limestone. The places where the limestone layer has fallen in to reveal the groundwater are perfect for a refreshing bathe and for diving and snorkelling. The animal life of the Yucatán is also very unusual. In the jungle there are puma, ocelot, jaguar, red deer, crocodile and iguana as well as snakes and insects like scorpions and tarantulas. The abundant birdlife includes flamingoes, toucans, parrots and humming-birds.

A stretch of the new Mex 307 motorway, under construction between Cancún and Tulum, runs straight through the Xel-Ha archaeological zone. Two trucks belonging to the I.N.A.H. (Instituto Nacional de Antropologia e Historia) are parked beside the road. At dusk there is hectic activity here; people are digging, sieving and sorting. In the evening sun Graciela, the archaeologist, stands on a spoil-heap many feet high and wipes the sweat from her brow. She shrugs her shoulders resignedly: "What we have here is a Mayan settlement, a small town with several tombs and ceremonial buildings. But it's such a tragedy! In a week's time the bulldozers will arrive and destroy everything, before we have time to make a proper investigation and inventory."

Experts reckon that there are still more than 11,000 undiscovered Mayan cultural sites, hidden in the undergrowth, all over Mexico.

Only with special permission from the INAH, and by paying a high entrance fee, are we allowed to visit Tulum - the City of the Sunrise - before the normal opening-time of 9 a.m. At 6 a.m. it is still dark and deserted. The rocks and walls give off the heat of the previous day and warm us in the cool dawn air. (S.21) In the uncanny silence it is scarcely imaginable that 500 years ago,

when the Spanish arrived, there was still a bustling life here; and that as the sun rose from the sea, it was greeted by the voices and sounds of men and beasts, bringing the day to life. The picturesque fortified city on the edge of the Caribbean has 800,000 visitors every year and its temples are the most-photographed tourist attraction in the Yucatán.

Tourists seldom, if ever, find their way to San Francisco Aké. Here the Mayas live as farmers, just as they have always done. For thousands of years they have worked their fields with machete and shovel and planted maize, pumpkin and beans. They build their traditional houses of wood and cover the roof with palm-leaves or straw. They all speak Maya, and only concepts which do not exist in their native language are expressed in Spanish.

The village pays great respect to the Itzá family. Juan José Itzá is a priest and leader of the Kruso Ob, the "Church of the Speaking Cross." He and his brother Santiago are also the best-known curanderos - Mayan faith-healers - in the whole of Quintana Roo. Pastora, Juan José's 20-year-old granddaughter, is the only Spanish-speaker in the family; she is the link between two worlds, those of yesterday and of tomorrow.

In 1850, during the Caste War, when the Mayas rebelled against the occupying Spanish decendants of the original colonists, the miracle of the Speaking Cross occurred for the first time. It promised the expulsion of all white men from paradise and exhorted the Mayas to resist. To this day it symbolizes the faith in the prophesy of liberation, it gives strength to the Mayas and protects them against the foreigner. Mayan priests are demanding the return of the cities of their forefathers, their holy places which are today the playground of archaeologists and tourists alike.

The life of the Mayas is strongly influenced by Catholicism but the belief in the gods and spirits of their ancestors is held deep in their hearts, and in many villages ancient rituals have survived. The Mayas regard modern Mexico with distrust.

At the age of seven Santiago began the apprenticeship of a Mayan healer with his father. Now he is 81 and the little man with a crippled leg claims he is still learning. He holds in his head the combinations of over 800 different substances from herbs and plants; he feels his patient's pulse and murmurs prayers. He stirs potions and salves but also pronounces the sacred formulae for summoning the much-needed rain. He makes sacrifices to put the spirits in a favourable mood. In his hut a cross stands, a holy candle burns and there is a smell of incense. His secret aids to healing include a burnt-out bulb from a truck's headlamp, stones and a silver coin. The aim of Mayan natural medicine is to bring body and soul once more into harmony. The success of the shamans is well-documented and the traditional healers and their methods have been recognized by Mexico's social insurance system.

The further south we journey, the more lush the vegetation becomes. Hidden in the forest, close to the border with Belize, lies the little township of Tres Garantías. In the house of Dona Olga, the town's only restaurant, the tables are decorated with banknotes from the USA, Britain, France, Germany and Switzerland under a protective sheet of plastic. For Olga and the people of Tres Garantías 1989 was a special year. They were visited by a group of international experts, whose advice on the conservation and better exploitation of the tropical forest was sorely needed. The villagers depend on the forest for their livelihood. They work as tree-fellers, hunters and as gatherers of honey and chicle. The raw material for chewing-gum, chicle comes from the sap of the zapote tree, a native species which is only found in Yucatán. In ancient times the Mayas used the sap to make balls for playing games, but the trees are now threatened by the wholesale felling of tropical hardwood. "Only if the forest is intact can chicle grow - if too many mahogany-trees are cut down, there will be no more chicle," says Pascal, proud to have been a chiclero for the past 36 years.

The chicleros' work is extremely dangerous and exhausting. The white sap only flows in the rainy season, from January to June, from cuts made in the bark of the zapote-trees. The jungle is full of puma and other ferocious "big cats", three kinds of poisonous snake live in the tree-tops and the air is thick with billions of mosqitoes. A particular species of fly, which lays its larvae in human ears, causes the "chiclero's ulcer." Working in small groups, they use their machetes to hack a narrow path for up to 20 km (12 miles) through the lush, steaming jungle greenery. Bathed in sweat, they set up a primitive camp with a palapa for the hammocks and a fire to boil the chicle. (S.23) Every evening the harvested sap is boiled down to a thick gum for up to four hours,

then shaped into 10 kilo (5 lb) blocks. For one or two weeks the whole area within a radius of 4km (2.4 miles) is combed for chicozapote-trees that have not been tapped for at least seven years. The trees reach a height of 15m (50 ft) and are climbed with bare hands and feet, and only the aid of a rope. A channel is cut into the bark of the trunk and the sap is caught in a bag at the foot of the tree. The largest amount of sap comes from the thickest, century-old trees, but even they only produce two kilos (4 lb). "As a young man I used to collect sixty kilos a week, but now I am fifty-one and only manage twenty-five kilos. That is a lot of work for very little money, because at the moment we only get twenty pesos per kilo." The boom time for chicle is past, but until the 1930s it brought steady work for many, and wealth and prosperity for quite a few people in Quintana Roo. Now that chewing-gum is manufactured chemically, the price of chicle is dictated by Japanese industry.

he enormous sums that are paid for stolen Mayan art-treasures are something a poor chiclero can only dream about. Countless cultural treasures lie buried or overgrown by the jungle: thousand-year-old Mayan ruins, temples and tombs. Men in search of a quick buck have come to plunder with pickaxes, sledge-hammers and chain-saws, and cause incalculable damage. They leave behind nothing but piles of rubble, useless to archaeologists and lost for ever to posterity. Although grave-robbers face the most severe punishment in Mexico, the Museum of Anthropology calculates that some 300 works of art leave Mexico illegally every day.

t took the Mexicans a very long time to realize that a fortune lay in the beaches of Quintana Roo, on the almost deserted Caribbean coast of Yucatán and its offshore islands. In 1969 an elaborate plan was worked out on the drawing-board for a tourist town, the perfect holiday factory. It was to be on the island of Cancún, 21 km (12.6 miles) long, 400m (1/4 mile) across at its widest point and with only 126 inhabitants. Since then hotels have soared skywards like contemporary pyramids. Half-a-million migrants from all over Mexico and the rest of the world have come to fight for a living in Mexico's tourist capital. Today the tourist sector is the biggest employer and still growing. This giant beach resport, born in a test-tube as it were, is continuously expanding. It is one gigantic money-machine. Of the 3 million tourists in the whole of Yucatán, 2.6 million - mainly from the USA - come to Cancún. Statistically they spend on average 5.2 nights in one of the 28,000 beds and spend about US$1,200 during their stay. Everything is designed to make Americans feel at home. Here they can eat at MacDonald's, the Hard Rock Café, Planet Hollywood, the Rainforest Café, Ruth's Steak-House and so on. Even the prices are shown in familiar dollars and cents. The entertainment dynamo runs at full revs round the clock, with Caribbean Night, Fiesta Mexicana, Miss Bikini, Mister Cancún...there's never a dull moment. It's a promise!

Charter flights land and take off continually at Cancún's international airport. On a day-trip to the island of Holbox Bruce Montes flies over the tourist metropolis. From a height of 1,000 ft Cancún looks small and vulnerable. The hotels stand huddled close together on the narrow coral strip between lagoon and sea. No longer do the waves break on a broad, white beach since Hurricane Gilbert slimmed it down severely in 1988. Instead, in many places they lick hungrily at the concrete foundations of the hotels.

A pirate's lair, a fishing-village, a bird-watcher's paradise, a beach with no gringos and no air-conditioned luxury. More sand than you could ever wish for, calm waters, a heaven for shell-collectors. We have come back to nature - on the little island of Holbox off the north coast of Yucatán, between the Caribbean and the Gulf of Mexico. From Cancún it is only 20 minutes by air and we fly over a gently curving bay, 30 km (18 miles) wide, with a deserted beach of white sand. The Cessna is on familiar territory when it lands, because the airstrip is the private property of the man who owns Sweden's Saab Aircraft company. The edges of the sandy track are decorated with shells, and two dogs wag their tails happily. The village consists of typical Caribbean houses, built of wood and painted in glowing colours, their windows and doors wide open. The islanders greet us in a friendly style, looking us straight in the eye. The visitors, who are predominantly Mexicans and Europeans, are warmly welcomed on Holbox and provide a pleasant diversion for the inhabitants of this idyllic, unspoilt haven. Holbox is like Cancún and Playa used to - 30 years ago.

Marion Friedel

PLAYA DEL CARMEN

ADVANCED. DIVE MASTER
SCUBA DIVING
1 tank
2 tank
RESORT COURSE
NIGHT DIVE

MODA CASUAL
SISTEMA DE APARTADO
BLUSAS
FALDAS
VESTIDOS

BILLARES
EL TIGRE

Carniceria

WELCOME TO
BAR
RESTAURANT
BREAKFAST

LONCHERIA
LAS
PALMAS

Hotel
Playa Suites
DAILY
WEEKLY
MONTHLY

Panaderia del Caribe

Hotel
Hacienda María Bonita

POSADA
MURALLA

AVENTURA
MEXICANA
RESORT & BAR
A/C.T.V. FRIDGE
LARGE POOL, HOT JACUZZI
RESTAURANT-BAR
JARDIN TROPICAL
BREAKFAST-LUNCH-DINNER
HOTEL
APARTMENT
MONTHLY
FOR RENT
VACANCY
30%
off
FOR RENT
FORD

IEEA

COZUMEL MEXICO
THE BEST
BRAIDS
WRAPS
TRENZAS
Playa
PalanCaR

BI NVENIDOS
WELCOME
ADMI STRACION PORTUARIA
API
COZUMEL, Q. ROO, MEXICO
CANACO
ROLEX
FAT TUESDAY
TICKETS TO:
BOLETOS A:
PLAYA DEL CARMEN
HERE

FIESTA MEXICANA

Bird-man from Papantla

Flamenco dancers at the Hotel Iberostar-Tucan - Playacar

Bottle-dance in Chichen-Itzá

Bull-fight in Colosio - Playa del Carmen

Distorting mirrors mounted on wheels

El Alabado - a dance from Michoacán

Musicians from Vera Cruz

Bird-men from Papantla

Folk-dancing in Mérida

Mariachis in the Pericos - Cancún

Mayan costumes in Valladolid

Dancer from Mérida

Papier-maché in Playa del Carmen

Monastery church - Izamal

The main market in Mérida

La Bamba - the dance from Vera Cruz

Disco Center in Cancún

Candy-floss - fiesta in Playa del Carmen

Sunday in Mérida

Tracer

LARGA DISTANCIA

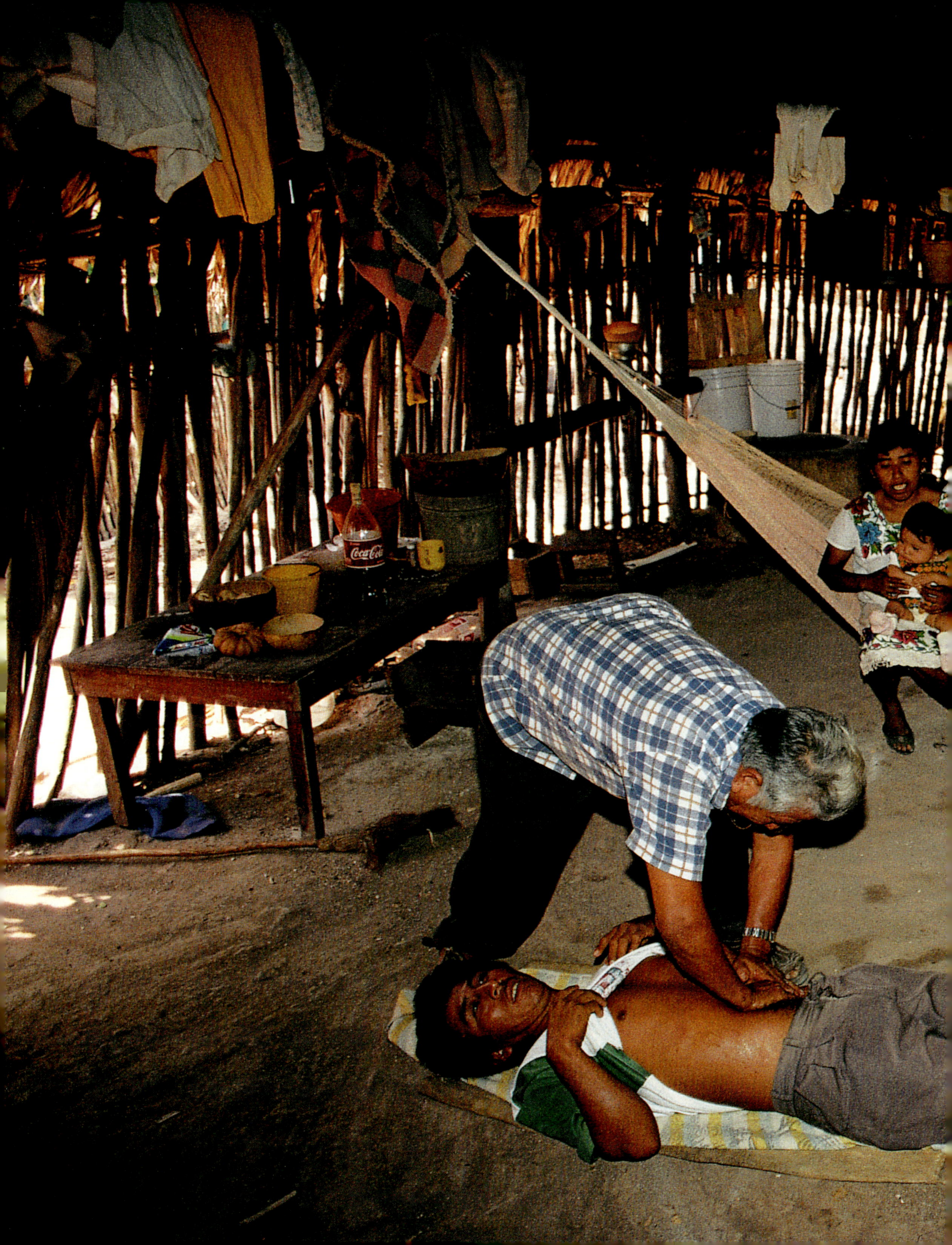
Coca-Cola

The Riviera Maya - a new and exotic holiday destination. Is this just a creative concept? Something dreamed up by the advertising men? Well, in a way it is. Especially if you equate creativity with art and culture. It's all about holidays, relaxation and new experiences. To bathe on the Caribbean coast of Mexico's Yucatán peninsula, and visit the ancient sites of Mayan civilization, all on the same day - the combination could well be unique. And here I am not thinking so much of student backpacking but of comfortable beach holidays combined with fascinating excursions to excavation sites. The Mexican state of Quintana Roo invested heavily in this rapid tourism development. A completely new infrastructure was built, with roads, harbours and airports. Alongside the traditional tourist centres on the island of Cozumel and the Isla Mujeres, three more holiday regions were created - on the drawing-board.

In the 1970s came Cancún, then in the late 1990s the Riviera Maya, from Cancún to Tulum and now, scheduled for the year 2000, the Costa Maya from Tulum to Xcalak.

These new holiday centres have been built on a deserted coastline, which means that no local inhabitants have had to be relocated. This is how the holiday landscape is currently taking shape and may well become one of the world's largest holiday destinations. The conditions are ideal: along the 400 km (240 mile) coast from Cancún to Xcalak one beautiful beach follows another. The ultra-modern hotel complexes and resorts offer every standard, from independent to all-inclusive. Added to that are the long hours of sunshine and first-class water-sports facilities. The hotel buildings, seldom more than three storeys high, stand in well-tended tropical gardens; sometimes a patch of virgin forest has been incorporated into them. So you can stroll through the jungle on the way from the hotel restaurant to the pool. Of course, it is everyone's privilege to laze around to their heart's content on holiday. But if you never leave your hotel on the Caribbean coast of Quintana Roo, you will sadly take home little of the fascination of Yucatán. I have visited the country nearly 40 times and each time I have discovered a new chapter in the history and culture of the Mayas. Every year new secrets are brought to light and holidaymakers in Yucatán can witness them at first hand. I doubt whether this is true anywhere else in the world. To give you just one example; the temple complex in Tulum, one of the finest anywhere, was built by the Mayas on top of a cliff. Below it stretches a dream of a beach.

The history of the Mayas has fascinated me since my very first visit to Mexico - and if I am honest, it means more to me than the white beaches and crystal-clear waters of the Caribbean. This culture still holds many secrets. Did you know that in Mexico, and in the neighbouring countries of Belize and Guatemala, 7.5 million Maya people still live and that they speak 31 different languages? Even before the rise of Greece and Rome, the ancestors of today's Mayas had created an empire with cities, palaces, monuments and pyramids. Where today there is only impenetrable jungle, they had an intensive agriculture with an elaborate irrigation system, and the major population centres were linked by paved roads.The healing arts of the Mayas and their knowledge of herbal medicine still have applications today; more and more patients are being cured by ancient Mayan therapy. And the Mayan calendar was more precise than any that has ever been used in Europe. Their script was one of the most astonishing intellectual achievements of any of the Amerindian peoples.

It bears no relation whatever to the western alphabet. We know this because experts have finally succeeded in deciphering about 85 per cent of the ancient Mayan script. One of those responsible for this dazzling achievement was the Russian linguistic scientist Yuri Knorosov from St Petersburg - a brilliant theoretician who, believe it or not, has never set foot on Mexican soil.

The last independent Mayan kingdom was subjugated by the Spanish in 1697. Since then this advanced Central American culture has slumbered beneath the virgin forest. It is thought that in Yucatán about 2,000 Mayan sites still lie hidden in the jungle. So far, it is calculated that only between two and eight per cent of them have been exposed. Recently some of the ruins have been located by satellite photography. This of course costs a great deal of money, and that is why the archaeologists are so glad to see people visiting the Mayan cultural sites. The entrance charges they pay also provide financial support for their ambitious excavation programme.

Knut Wehner

PLAYA

Body-painting

Caracol

Playa del Carmen

Playa del Carmen, El Faro beach

Playacar hotel zone

I first visited the Caribbean coast of the Yucatán peninsula over forty years ago. Since then Quintana Roo has changed beyond recognition! In 1963 I stayed in a fisherman's hut on the Isla Mujeres and Cancún was uninhabited. In Cancún's big lagoon, where today jet-skis skim over the water, we caught langoustes with our bare hands in the calm, clear water, made a fire and cooked them in a tin bucket with a little lemon-juice. Tourists were still a rarity in the Mayan temple sites and there was not an attendant to be seen. Where there are now barriers, I was then able to clamber about and take photographs unhindered. Today one requires endless expensive permits from Mexico City, which can only be made use of on site with the addition of a hefty tip. Without a permit you cannot even take a tripod into the ruins.

By 1973, ten years after my first visit, the island of Cozumel had already become a charter destination. My wife and I, accompanied by Rudolf Bittorf, who was a tour guide in those days, sailed down the coast from Cancún to Tulum in a replica pirate-ship. Concrete shells of the first hotels were appearing in Cancún, and on the deserted Punta Maroma we caught our own fish, including a huge barracuda, and grilled them on a camp-fire.

For Rudolf Bittorf this expedition was the turning-point of his life. He remained in Mexico, got married there and is today the owner of excursion-boats, authentic replicas of sailing-ships from the time of Christopher Columbus.

Nowhere in the world have I seen such headlong acceleration in tourism. From zero to full speed by 2005. And everything perfectly organized and fully functioning!

Marion Friedel - Cancún under construction in 1974

We drive around a great deal on the new motorways. On the once deserted coast of Cancún there is now a long parade of hotels, and all the famous temple ruins are fenced off and guarded.

Rudolf, who owns Colón Tours and is also Honorary German Consul, holds the key to our rediscovery of Yucatán. In a Colón Tours minibus, Avelardo the driver chauffeurs us tirelessly, safely and dependably all over the country. The peninsula is flat from end to end. So that I can photograph the beaches from an interesting angle, my equipment includes a telescopic ladder. With Avelardo supporting the ladder I can double my height in an instant.

Also with me on this trip I carry 50 kilos (100 lb) of diving equipment. I wonder whether the diving off Cozumel is still as good as it was 30 years ago; or has it all been ruined? Far from it - the diving grounds are better than ever. They are swarming with fish, which love being fed with tortillas by the snorkellers.

I take a lot of my photos in Colosio, the poor, working-class district of Playa del Carmen. Tourists never stray into this area, and the inhabitants, illegal settlers from all over Mexico, start by asking me with friendly concern: "Are you looking for a wife, or do you just need a room for the night?"

It is not until we are up in a light aircraft, at an altitude of roughly 2,000 to 3,000 ft, that we can recognize the characteristic landscape of Yucatán. After some initial misunderstandings, the pilot, Bruce Montes, and I have developed a sign-language; because, with the door open the noise of wind and engine makes verbal communication impossible. Not every day brings ideal weather for photography. The many bush-fires sometimes reduce visibility to less than 1,000 yards. Mist, smoke and rain make many trial shots necessary. After 21 hours of flying-time, and 50 take-offs and landings, we have become a perfect team.

Rudolf Bittorf

Michael Friedel Avelardo, our driver
the telescopic ladder Xpu-ha

Michael Friedel Chankanaab

Michael Friedel - supermarket - Playa del Carmen

In the south, beyond Chetumal, the jungle becomes ever denser and taller. Accompanied by Ernesto Parra Calderón from the Ministry of Tourism we were looking for Mayan ruins near Dos Aguadas, and after a sweltering 10km (6 mile) trek along overgrown jungle paths, we found them.
I was glad to have Minolta's professional back-up service on this trip. After flying in a single-engined Cessna with no doors, and diving in caves, the dust and water had taken a heavy toll on my five Minolta Dynax 7. There were times when three of them were out of action. Twice I ordered new supplies to be air-freighted in. Luckily my eight lenses, from 15mm to 400mm, stayed the course.
Our base was the Hotel El Faro in Playa del Carmen. The creator and owner of the lighthouse and its associated hotel is an old friend from Munich named Bernd Dürrmeier. But the first man from Munich to open a hotel in Playa is the fashion designer Rolf Albrecht. He got up at six in the morning to join me on my photo-tour of the old colonial city of Mérida.
To make new friends among the Mayas requires a great deal of patience, tact and sensitivity. You have to earn their friendship with persistence and the presentation of gifts on every visit. Only after four visits, each of which required four long days' travelling, were we allowed to allowed to photograph the Mayan healer, Juan José Itzá, and his family in their village home. The villagers want to have nothing to do with foreigners and tourists. During Easter Week we witnessed their deep religious belief and their great poverty. Their fields yield barely enough for them to live on. This book won the "Lente de Plata", Mexico's first prize for colour photography, which was presented to me by President Ernesto Zedillo.

Capt. Bruce Montes, pilot - Aero-Saab - Holbox airport

Ernesto Parra Calderón - the jungle near Tres Garantías - Quintana Roo

INWARD FLIGHTS

To Cancún: direct from Europe with British Airways, LTU, Condor, Martin Air, Lauda Air. Changing at Mexico City, with BA, Air France, Lufthansa, KLM - onward flights with Mexicana or Aeromexico. From the USA, with American Airlines, Continental, United Airlines and Mexicana.

CUSTOMS AND IMMIGRATION

Visitors from the EU require a **passport** valid for at least a further 6 months, and a **tourist card** The latter are generally issued by the airline. Children's travel documents must carry a photograph. The tourist card is normally valid for 30 days and should be carried with you at all times. It is a two-part form which is stamped on arrival. The top copy is for entry and the second copy for departure. If it is lost or you require an extension, contact your country's embassy or consulate in Mexico as well as the Mexican immigration authorities. **Foodstuffs** may **not** be brought into the country. The following items can be brought in **duty-free**: 50 cigars, 200 cigarettes or up to 250 grams of tobacco; also 3 litres of wine, cameras, video™cameras, film, cassettes and medications for personal use. In addition you may bring in gifts up to a value of US$500. There is an **export ban** on archaeological finds and antiquities unless an official permit has been obtained.

CURRENCY

The Mexican currency is the **peso**; following the recent currency reform it is officially the nuevo peso (N$). There are 100 centavos to the peso. Note that the sign for the peso is the same as for the dollar ($) and the "N" is often omitted, so this can lead to confusion since, or international guidance, the US dollar is often quoted as well. It is best to change your money at a bank or at a bureau de change (casa de cambio) run by a bank. **US dollar travellers cheques** are the safest method of payment, as other currencies can only be changed in the larger towns, and then only at a poor exchange rate. The major credit cards are accepted in most hotels and in larger restaurants and shops. **Caution**: pick-pockets are very skilful in Mexico - especially in tourist centres - so you should never carry large amounts of cash with you.

MEDICINE

If you are arriving directly from Europe no vaccinations are required. But in tropical regions **malaria** is quite common, and an injection is advisable if you plan to spend any length of time away from the beaten track (especially in the rain-forest). **AIDS** is very widespread in Mexico. Animals should be avoided, as they may carry **rabies**. Should you need medical attention, try the hotel staff first. Doctors and medication normally have to be paid for in cash. You are very strongly advised to take out **travel health insurance**. Most common medicines can be bought at a farmacia without a prescription. However, if you require specific personal medication you should bring an adequate supply with you from home.

HOTELS

The choice of hotels is very wide and varied. Most of the big hotels in **Cancún's** hotel zone and on the Riviera Maya between Cancún and Tulum are right on the beach. On the **Riviera Maya** particularly there are a growing number of **hotel complexes** which operate on the **„all- inclusive"** principle. But in Cancún, too, the number of these resorts is increasing. The independent holidaymaker can choose between a top-notch **luxury hotel** (from US$250 per night upwards), a **first class hotel** (from US$150), then mid-range, tourist class and small **private hotels** (US$25-75), right down to the **hoteles familiares** and **casas de huespedes**, which are no more than guesthouses (under US$25). **Posadas** may either be mid-range or tourist class hotels. In Yucatán a new type of accommodation is springing up: hotels are being opened which have been converted, usually with good taste and style, from old **sisal haciendas** (from US$300 per night). For people who want to stay for a longer period a good idea is the so-called **aparthotel** with kitchenette and refrigerator (from US$65). Tourism is busy all year round but the **high season** is from November until Easter.

RELIGION

More than 90% of the yucateos are Catholic and in country areas particularly the people are deeply religious. Church services are still well-attended. But it is a naive and simple faith containing many essentially pre-Christian elements, a complete blending of Catholic and indigenous rites, symbols and concepts. The cult of the Virgin Mary enjoys special popularity.

ISLAND TRANSPORT AND EXCURSIONS

Ferry connections: **Puerto Juarez - Isla Mujeres**: passenger ferry, 20-minute crossing, 8-12 times a day in both directions. **Playa del Carmen - Cozumel**: Passenger ferry, 45-minute crossing, 8-12 times a day in both directions. **Puerto Morelos - Cozumel**: Car ferry, 120-minute crossing, once a day in both directions. Planned onwards: **Puerto Morelos - Cuba**. A variety of excursions are offered by the hotels and local travel agencies. We recommend the agencies GO MEXICO TOURS and COLÓN TOURS.

TELEVISION, PRESS AND BOOKS

The larger hotels usually offer a round-the-clock TV programme via **cable** and **satellite**, and several American movie channels are also available. On **medium wave and UHF radio** numerous stations broadcast all kinds of music, from rock and pop to Latin-American rhythms and mariachi bands. The BBC World Service can be picked up with a good international receiver. Throughout Mexico you can buy the local English-language paper, "The News". European newspapers and magazines can generally be found in the shops of larger hotels and in branches of the Sanborn department store chain.

ELECTRICITY

The main supply is 110 volt/ 60hz alternating current. Plugs and sockets are of the US type, so, if you are coming from Europe, do not forget to bring an adaptor with you.

CLOTHING AND EQUIPMENT

For beach and bathing holidays in the Cancún region we recommend light summer clothing. For summer evenings you will need long trousers and **mosquito-repellant**, as the insects are particularly active around dusk. Wear a hat to prevent sunstroke, and do not forget to take **protective sun-cream**. The Mexican dress-code, especially in country districts, is rather conservative. In churches and in the better restaurants you may well be turned away if you are wearing shorts or other revealing garments. When visiting archaeological sites, you should wear strong, comfortable shoes with thick soles. Since many hotels and restaurants, especially in Cancún, have air-conditioning adjusted to suit American tastes **ice-cold**, it is always advisable to have a light shawl, scarf or jacket with you.

TELEPHONE

Telephoning to and from Mexico is expensive. Long-distance calls from hotels can cost at least £17.50/US$ 26 for 3 minutes, and this is often the minimum charge, even for shorter calls. In some places you have to pay this sum even if you have only obtained the ringing-tone but no conversation has taken place. Recently, **coin- and card-phones** (Ladatel) have become available for international calls. In country districts you will still find the **casetas de larga distancia** for manually connected long-distance calls. When dialling direct to Europe, you must first dial 00, then the country prefix (e.g. 44 for the UK), then the number, omitting the initial zero.

CAR-HIRE, TAXIS AND BUSES

Hiring a car locally is relatively expensive. It is more economical to book your car before you leave home, with an international firm like Avis, Hertz or Budget. Active participation in Mexico's road traffic requires a considerable degree of re-education. In the country regions of the Yucatán peninsula traffic density is not high. But Cancún and other large cities such as Mérida and Campeche are very different. At a road junction you should always reckon on traffic coming from both right and left, even when the lights are in your favour. Legalistic insistence on your right of way only gets you into trouble in Mexico. Pay attention to speed limits, because you will be easily recognized as a **gringo**, and every policeman will be glad to supplement his meagre salary with a little **mordida** (which is really a bribe but is considered as a kind of toll or fine). In towns and villages the speed-limit is 40 kph (24 mph), and on open highways it is 80 kph (48 mph). Driving at night should be avoided for a variety of reasons. To hire a car you will always require a credit-card. A driving-license from your own country is sufficient. **Petrol (gas) stations** are usually found only at infrequent intervals, and they only accept cash. If you prefer to let someone else do the driving, you can take **busses** without difficulty to the remotest corners of the peninsula. Tourists are advised to travel first-class in air-conditioned busses which also have an on-board toilet. These busses only stop in major towns and cities and reserved seats can be obtained by going to the ticket-office in person (not by telephoning). In addition to these, there are second- and third-class busses. Even pigs and chickens are allowed to travel on these. For short journeys it is best to use a t**axi, communal taxi** (colectivo) or

CLIMATIC TABLE

	Jan.	March	May	July	Sept.	Nov.
Average max. daytime temperature in °C.	**28**	**29**	**33**	**33**	**30**	**29**
Average min. nighttime temperature in °C.	**17**	**18**	**22**	**23**	**22**	**19**
Average daily hours of sunshine	**6**	**7**	**8**	**8**	**6**	**7**
Average rainy days per month	**4**	**3**	**8**	**10**	**12**	**5**

minibus. Cancún is divided up into taxi-zones. A scale of fares is displayed in the hotel, or can be obtained from reception. Even so, you should always agree the fare with the driver before getting into a taxi and make sure, by insisting if necessary, that the taximeter is switched on (assuming there is one).

SPORT AND LEISURE

Diving and snorkelling. Of all places, **Cozumel** is made for divers. It's diving-waters are among the most famous and interesting in the Caribbean. It's **reefs** include the **Palancar, Chancanaab, Colombia** and **Maracaibo**. Both in the hotels and also in the friendly little town of Cozumel there many professional diving-schools offering courses, diving tours and the necessary equipment. In Cancún and Playa del Carmen there are numerous water-sport and diving bases in hotels, on the beach and in the towns, which offer snorkelling expeditions and diving-courses, as well as **water-skiing, wave-runners, catamarans and blue-water fishing**. To dive in the subterranean **cenotes** a special diving certificate is necessary. Advice and information is obtainable from **Aquatech**, whose address is **Villas Derosa, Aventuras Akumal tel./fax 987 590 20**. There are facilities for **windsurfing** and **para-sailing** on the beach at many hotels. **Golf in Cancún**: The luxury Pok-Ta-Pok course (18 holes, designed by Robert Trent) is on a spit of land jutting into the Nichupte Lagoon. The 12th hole lies among Mayan ruins and there is a pleasant restaurant. At the luxury Caesar's Park hotel there is another 18-hole course. **Golf in Playa del Carmen**: an 18-hole course. **Tennis**: in the tourist centres nearly all the hotels have their own tennis-courts on which non-residents are allowed to play, provided they are invited by a hotel guest.

FILMING AND PHOTOGRAPHY

In archaeological sites, museums and public buildings you require a **special permit** in order to take still photographs with flash or tripod, or to use a 16mm cine-camera. Video filming is allowed on payment of a charge of US$10. As a rule the permit can be obtained at the entrance to each site. Film is relatively expensive in Mexico and you are only allowed to bring in 10 rolls per person. On the other hand developing is quick and very cheap. As in any country you should respect people's privacy. The Mayas are particularly hard to photograph.

FOOD AND DRINK

There is no denying that Mexican cuisine - most of it anyway - is enormously rich in calories. There are three reasons for this. Firstly, the basic nutritious ingredients of nearly every Mexican meal are **sweet-corn** and **beans**. Secondly the various ways of serving avocado (e.g. guacamole) are little "calorie-bombs". Thirdly, we must not conceal the fact that Mexicans are unused to frying in coated pans with a small amount of oil. Instead delicacies as **flautas, quesadillas** and **tostadas** are sizzled in pork fat until crisp, and are brought to the table with delicious fillings. However, the real reason why in Mexico you can so quickly achieve the national ideal of well-upholstered beauty, is that the food just tastes too good. The art of Mexican cooking grew from a blending of the simple, almost totally vegetarian dishes of the Aztecs, Mayas and other indigenous races, with the nourishing cooking brought over from Spain. Don't worry about the food being too hot and spicy! The dishes themselves are only lightly or moderately spiced. The real kick comes in the salsas and chilis, which are usually served on the side. The cuisine of Yucatán is in many respects different from that of the rest of Mexico, and has retained its own very independent character. These are some of the specialities: **Cochinita pibil** (pork) and **pollo pibil** (chicken), **poc-chuc, papadzules, huevos motulenos** and **sopa de lima**. Of course, you will find a lot of **fish** and **seafood dishes** on restaurant menus, and by the way, Yucatán brews its own beer. The term **refrescos** applies to chilled, non-alcoholic drinks like Coca-Cola, Pepsi-Cola, and lemonade, but not to fresh fruit squash. Freshly squeezed and undiluted fruit-juices are called **jugos**; if mixed with milk or water, they are **licuados**. The name **aguas frescas** conceals freshly puréed fuit mixed with tea or filtered water; but you should approach these elixirs with caution. The big, high-class hotels, especially in the tourist centres, now have water-purification plants (agua purificada). In the peninsula's country districts the hotels and restaurants keep bottles of pure, clean **drinking-water** on hand. In addition, you can buy delicious Mexican mineral waters (Tehuacan and Penafiel). One more thing: since a service-charge is not included in Mexican restaurant and hotel bills, it is usual to add a 10%-15% tip. Chambermaids should be tipped about US$1 for each day of your stay and porters about US$1 per piece of luggage. Taxi-drivers do not expect to be tipped except for special trips.

HOLIDAY SEASONS AND RAINY SEASONS

People here talk about a year of two seasons. The pleasantest and most beautiful time to take a holiday is in the northern winter (from November to April), when the daytime temperature is about 29° centigrade. From December to February the country can be seen in its fullest and finest bloom. It is pleasantly warm and occasionally hot, but not too damp. The hottest months are April, May and June. The rainy season lasts from June to September and is typified by heavy rain-showers, a lot of sultry and damp weather and swarms of mosquitoes. However, the rain never lasts very long. This is also the season of **hurricanes**. The average annual temperature on the peninsula is around 27° C. during the day, and seldom drops below 16°C. at night.

SOUVENIRS

The favourite souvenirs from Yucatán are hammocks, straw hats, huipiles (women's dresses), guayaberas (men's shirts), huaraches (leather sandals), ceramics and articles made from sisal, as well as filigree jewelry in gold and silver. In Mérida the panama hats and hammocks are of particularly good quality. In Cancún there are big American-style shopping-malls, with a large range of shops, as well as cafés and restaurants.

TIME

Mexico is divided into three time-zones. On the Yucatán peninsula Hora Centralapplies. This is 6 hours behind Greenwich Mean Time (GMT).

LANGUAGE

The national language is Spanish, but English is spoken in many hotels.

BOOKS ON DISCOVERY AND TRAVEL

Yucatán Peninsula, Insight Pocket Guides 1994
Yucatán Peninsula Handbook (5th Ed.)
Chicki Mallan, Moon Publications (California) 1994
Yucatán and Southern Mexico, Cadogan Books (UK) 1996
Yucatán's Maya Peasantry and the Origins of the Caste War
Terry Rugeley, Univ. of Texas Press 1996
Maya Civilization, T.P.Cuthbert, Smithsonian Institute 1993 Maya Road, J.Conrad, Bradt Country Guides (UK)
Maya Cosmos: Three Thousand Years on the Shaman's Path
David Freidel, Morrow, 1993 (US)
Maya for Travellers and Students: Guide to Language and Culture of Yucatán, Gary Bevington, Univ. of Texas Press, 1995
Archaeological Guide to the Yucatán Peninsula
Kelly, Univ, of Oklahoma Press 1993
Maya Art, Dynasty and Ritual, Thames & Hudson 1997 (US,UK)
Yucatán Cookbook: Recipes and Tales
Lyman Morton, Red Crane Books 1996 (US)

YUCATAN PENINSULA
N
50 km
30 miles~26 nautical miles
Gulf of Mexico
USA
MEXICO
GULF OF MEXICO
Miami
BAHAMAS
Mexico City
YUCATAN
Merida
Habana
CUBA
Cancun
DOM. REP.
HAITI
CARIBBEAN SEA
PAZIFIC OCEAN
SOUTH AMERICA
90°
89°
21°
20°
19°
18°
92°
91°
Dzilám de Bravo
Chicxulub
Puerto Progreso
Meteorit
Dzibilchaltún
MÉRIDA
IZAMAL
Celestun
Uman
Kantunil
Holca
Temozón Sur
Nature Reserve
Maxcanu
Mayapán
Tekit
Sotuta
Muna
Ticul
Teabo
Mani
UXMAL
Oxkutzcab
Sayil
Yayxhon
Tenabo
YUCATAN
Campeche
Hopelchen
EDZNA
Dzibalchen
Hochob
CAMPECHE
MEXICO
Calakmul Reserve
Sabancuy
Centenario
Laguna de Terminos
Ciudad del Carmen
Escárcega
Laguna Silvituc
Conhuas
Becan
Payan
Nicolas Bravo
Ruinas el Socorrito
Dos Aguadas
Tres Garantias
Palizada
TABASCO
Maya Biosphere Reserve
El Mirador
Rio Azul
GUATEMALA
TIKAL
International Airport
Nat. Airport
Pyramid
Monastery
Lighthouse
State Frontier
Inner Frontier
Reef
Nat. Park / Nat. Reserve
Adventure & Nature Park
Ocean Terminal Cruise Ships
Passenger Ferry

Geographical data on the Yucatán peninsula

Area: 142,000 sq.km (Mexico 1.98 million sq.km) divided into three federal states: Yucatán, Quintana Roo, Campeche.

State capitals: Mérida, Chetumal, Campeche.

Population: over 5 million, of which 25 % of mayan descent

Ethnis mix: Mestizos (mixed blood), Mayan and other indigenous races, white (Caucasian).

Religion: 90% Catholic

Language: Spanish, 25 Mayan languages

Political status: Mexico gained independence from Spain in 1821.

Currency: Mexican peso

Economy: Petroleum, tourism, sisal, fisheries in the Gulf of Mexico, hardwood, chicle chewing-gum, honey.

Special features: Zenotes - unterground rivers; world's fifth largest barrier reef, 250 km (150 miles) long from Isla Mujeres to Belize.

BOOKS PHOTOGRAPHED BY MICHAEL FRIEDEL

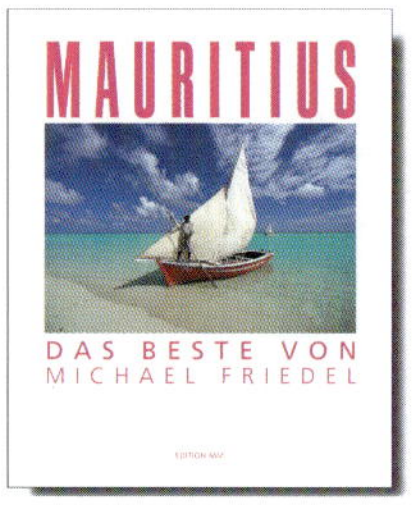

German

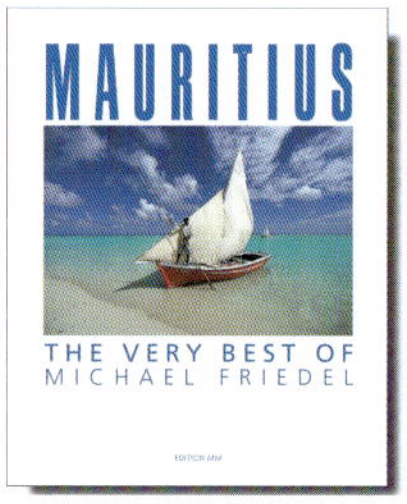

English

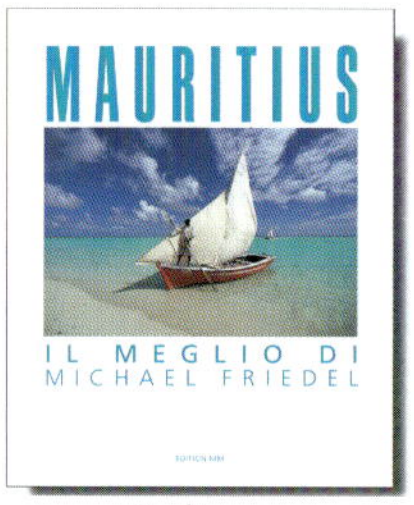

Italian

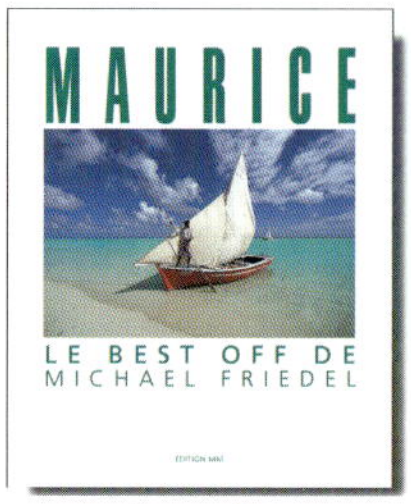

French

German

English

Italian

French

1 : 800 000

German

English

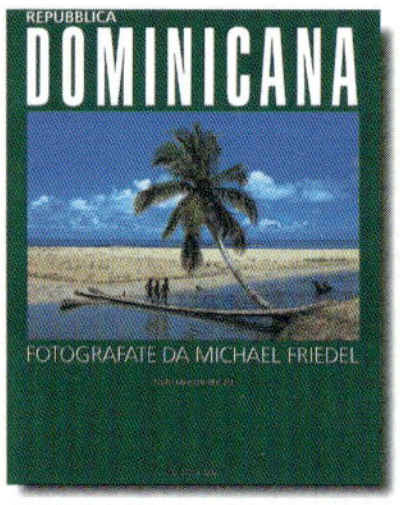

Italian

French

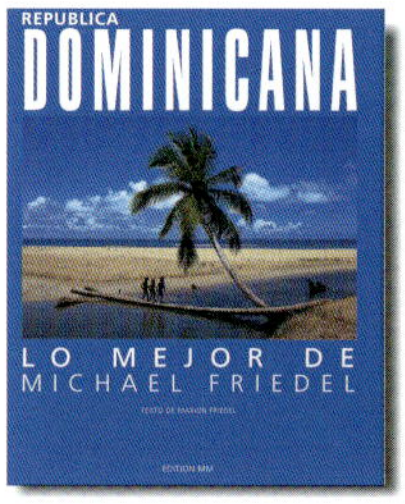

Spanish

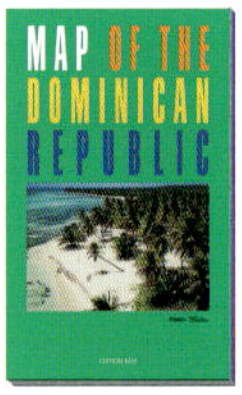

1 : 600 000

German

English

Italian

French

Spanish

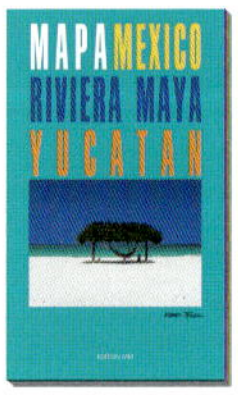

1 : 800 000

German

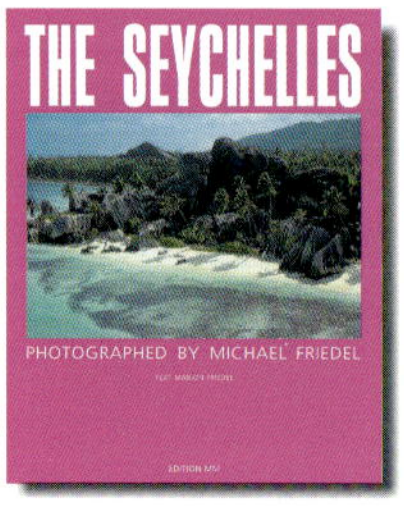

English

Italian

French

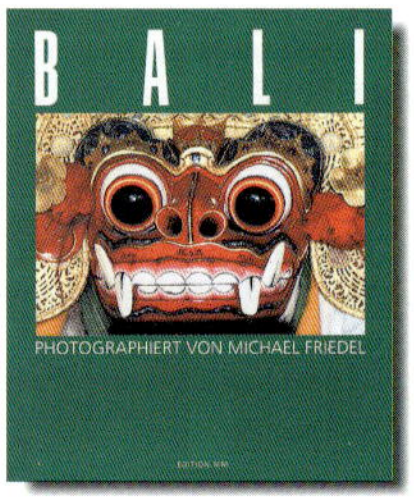

German

International: http://www.amazon.com; http://www.barnesandnobel.com; http://www.borders.com
Germany: www.amazon.de; **www.michael-friedel.de**; e-mail: info@michael-friedel.de
Austria: www.freytagberndt.com; **Canada**: www.edipresse.ca
France: Vilo Diffusion, 25, rue Ginoux, 75015 Paris, Fax: 01 45 79 97 15; **Swiss**: www.sbz.ch

Imprint
New, updated edition
First impression 2006; MM-Photodrucke GmbH, 83623 Steingau, Germany; Translated by Angus McGeoch; Concept: Marion & Michael Friedel
Photography: ©Michael Friedel; Titling and design: Stahl Grafikbüro, Munich; Repro: Franzis, Munich; Typesetting: Anita Huber, Deisenhofen
Maps: ©Thomas Braach, Munich; Printing and Binding: EGEDSA, Spain; ©Marion & Michael Friedel
ISBN 3-929489-41-4 / 978-3-929489-41-5 Printed in EU